Unseen Beauty
Mindful Stargazing and Astronomy

Table of Contents

Chapter 1. Introduction

Immerse yourself in the spectacular splendor of the universe with our Special Report - "Unseen Beauty: Mindful Stargazing and Astronomy". Dabble into a riveting journey that effortlessly combines the scientific wonders of astronomy with the meditative tranquility of mindfulness. This captivating report is far more than an informational guide; it's an inviting exploration that will transport you beyond the glimmering stars, spark your curiosity, and calm your mind. It's not about complex equations or intricate formulas, instead, it's a cheerful narration of our cosmic neighborhood that beckons the explorer within you. Ensuring each word evokes a sense of discovery and serenity, this special report is a treasure trove for novices and seasoned stargazers alike. Ignite your imagination, learn amidst tranquility, and realize the unseen beauty of the night sky that awaits you above. With this Special Report in your hands, every starry night will become an extraordinary celestial experience!

Chapter 2. The Cosmos: An Introduction to Mindful Stargazing

Firstly, let us transcend the confines of our earthly realm and traverse towards the vast expanse of the cosmos. As we leave behind the familiar sights of verdant landscapes and soothing seas, we find ourselves surrounded by the breathtaking grandeur of untouched, pervasive darkness. A seemingly endless vacuum, dotted with hypnotic celestial splendor. This, my dear reader, is our Universe; not a lifeless, soundless void, but a vibrant, ever-evolving expanse teeming with celestial activity.

2.1. Embracing the Silence

Silence is a rare luxury on Earth, often lost beneath the constant humdrum of our modern world. Above, amidst the cosmos, silence is a beautiful enigma. Its pure, unwavering, and absolute. Rather than presenting silence as an absence of sound, stargazing invites us to perceive it as the intact harmonics of a celestial symphony. We hear not with our ears, but with our minds.

As we gaze into the night sky, senses simmering with heightened awareness, mindfulness guides us to bask in this serenity. Notice the tranquillity that the silence brings; let it envelop your being. This is the majestic ambience of the cosmos - silence rendered into pure symphony.

2.2. Bathing in Starlight

We are often so ensnared by the artificial lights around us that we forget the true illumination - the soft, gentle radiance of countless stars. Each star – distant and indiscernible – provides a unique splendor to the nighttime tapestry. Just like the variety in a box of chocolates, each star differs from the next.

Turn off the distractions, allow your eyes to adjust, and train them onto the seemingly endless depths above. The more you invite your vision to roam freely about, the more the universe will reward with a celestial spectacle. Be aware of these tiny sparks of brilliance, their varying color and intensity. Let go of your desire to classify these stars as mere objects; instead, embrace their individuality – acknowledge their existence; immerse yourself in their radiance.

2.3. Finding Connection in Constellations

Stargazing is more than a simple pursuit of astronomical knowledge. It's a portal to our past, a connection to our ancestors who, for millennia, have found guidance from the stars. Constellations – patterns formed by stars – are etchings on this cosmic canvas, steeped in mythology and cultural significance.

Let your eyes trace these ancient patterns in the sky. Recognize them, not by their scientific names but by the stories they are part of. Orion, the great hunter. Cassiopeia, the vain queen. Scorpius, the deadly scorpion. Each constellation has a tale to tell, a legacy to behold. And as you engage yourself in these celestial stories, you weave yourself into the timeless tapestry of the cosmos.

2.4. The Dance of the Planets

While stars are the permanent residents of the cosmos, the planets play their part in the grand performance too. These wayward travelers of the solar system have a rhythm to their appearances. Mercury, Venus, Mars, Jupiter, and Saturn – each, at its own pace, pirouetting across the star-studded stage.

Observe keenly and you'll spot the difference between a star and a planet. Planets don't twinkle; their light is steady compared to the stars, and often, they're the brightest objects in the sky after the Moon. A sense of wonder may fill your being as you realize that, despite the vast distance, you're looking at another world. Let this realization, this connection with the cosmic ballet, settle within you calmly.

2.5. The Galaxy: Our Stellar Abode

On a moonless night, away from the city lights, you'll witness something truly awe-inspiring - a thin luminescent band stretching across the sky; the Milky way – our home in the cosmos. This meandering river of light is a fellowship of billions of stars, glittering together in harmony.

Look closely, and you'll find contrasting elements within the band - bright patches, and darker spots. This is starlight and cosmic dust playing hide-and-seek. As your gaze rests on our galaxy, consider the scale of the cosmos, the stellar richness, and the astonishing fact that there exist countless galaxies beyond our own.

Stargazing is an orchestra of perception and imagination, seamlessly conducted by mindfulness. It's a feast for the senses, a balm for the soul, and above all, it's a gateway to the extraordinary universe we're a part of. As you continue to explore the night sky, remember: it's not an activity that's meant to evoke overwhelm; instead, it's an invitation into the tranquil cosmos, a subtle nudge to relinquish the frenetic pace of life momentarily - to just be and to savor the unseen beauty of the great celestial expanse. Let every cluster of stars, every visible planet, every shimmering galaxy, remind you of the moment you are living in; the chance to appreciate the cosmos above and the life within.

Chapter 3. Decoding the Night Sky: Constellations, Stars and Planets

Upon gazing at the night sky, you might perceive it as nothing more than a tapestry of twinkling stars strewn chaotically. However, astronomers have meticulously studied and mapped out these celestial bodies, creating a structured understanding of this seemingly tumultuous spectacle. Grasping the concept of the night sky can be slightly intimidating but immensely rewarding as well. This chapter will delve into an exhaustive exploration of understanding constellations, stars, and planets and learning to decode the startling expanse above us.

3.1. Deciphering Constellations

Observing the night sky, humans have, for millennia, connected the stellar dots into patterns, assigning them stories and names. These recognizable patterns of stars in the night sky are known as constellations. Thus, constellations serve as an elemental tool for celestial navigation and help us orient ourselves within the cosmic fabric.

You might have heard about the popular constellations like the Big Dipper, Orion's Belt, and Cassiopeia. It's fascinating to note how their appearance varies subtly across different latitudes and with time. The rotation of the earth, the changes in season, and the earth's position in its orbit around the sun affect the visibility of constellations. Meanwhile, circumpolar constellations (those positioned near a celestial pole) are visible throughout the year.

Learning the constellations can seem reminiscent of learning a new language, but with a little patience and consistent observation, the celestial sphere above will seem less enigmatic. Viewing constellations does not require a telescope. It's best begun with naked eye observations, clearly marking out the asterisms – easily recognizable star patterns within constellations – that frequently grace our night sky.

3.2. Expanding Your Stellar Knowledge: The Stars

Stars, the ubiquitous celestial objects lighting up the night canvas, are more than mere twinkling spheres. To observe the stars with intention is to understand our cosmic connections and origins. After all, we are made of star-stuff.

Every star has a life cycle, starting from its formation in nebulae, then evolving through sequences determined by their mass—culminating in outcomes such as white dwarfs, neutron stars, or black holes. Stars differ by size, temperature, color, and brightness. Their color—from red to white to blue—is an indicator of the star's surface temperature, while its brightness or magnitude depends on its inherent luminosity and distance from us.

Many stars are part of a system—binaries or multiples—bound together by gravitational interaction. Our sun, though often mistaken as the biggest star, is just a medium-size star. There are much larger stars out there, like Betelgeuse and Antares, known as supergiants.

Studying stars also leads us to the fascinating world of stellar spectroscopy, which allows us to identify the chemical composition of stars and help to decipher the mysteries of the universe.

3.3. A Tour of the Planets

Unlike stars that appear twinkling, planets shine with a steady light. Though they might seem alike to casual eyes, each planet in our solar system has distinctive features.

The inner planets, or terrestrial planets, – Mercury, Venus, Earth, and Mars – possess rocky surfaces. Outer planets, also known as gas giants – Jupiter, Saturn, Uranus, and Neptune – primarily consist of hydrogen and helium. The former two are often referred to as the 'Jovian Giants.' Furthermore, we also acknowledge one dwarf planet, formerly known as the ninth planet, intriguing Pluto.

Each planet orbits the sun at varying distances, resulting in differing lengths of 'years'. Planets also rotate on their axes, leading to the concept of a 'day'. Jupiter has the shortest day, completing one rotation in just under 10 hours.

By using a small telescope or even binoculars, one can see the rings of Saturn, the polar ice caps of Mars, or the Galilean moons of Jupiter.

There is much beauty and order amidst the seemingly chaotic cosmos. To study the night skies is not just a scientific pursuit but also a spiritual one. It is a humbling experience that evokes a sense of wonder and curiosity. So, arm yourself with a bit of knowledge, step out into the darkness, and let the universe unfold its secrets unto you.

Chapter 4. Equipment Essentials: Your Guide to Telescopes and Binoculars

Just as an amateur painter wouldn't attempt a masterpiece without the right brushes, amateur stargazers and aspiring astronomers need the correct tools to paint the canvases of their astronomical imaginations. Luckily, high-tech astronomical instruments aren't only for professionals; within your reach are tools that can transport you to a starscape full of celestial wonders, and it starts with an understanding of telescopes and binoculars.

4.1. Understanding the Basics

Telescopes and binoculars can be regarded as the astronaut's windows to the cosmos. They extend our vision, allowing us to observe celestial objects otherwise invisible to the unaided eye. The principle behind these tools is relatively simple: they gather and focus light. Just as a larger bucket can collect more rainwater, a larger lens or mirror (the "aperture") can gather more light from the sky, enabling you to peer deeper into the universe.

Telescopes come in various types, with each designed to perform a specific function and best suited to particular uses - a key aspect to bear in mind when deciding what to purchase. Binoculars are a more portable option that still offer a broad view of the heavens. Their simplicity and accessibility make them an excellent first step into observational astronomy.

4.2. Telescopes Unveiled

There are three main types of telescopes that entrance the stargazer:

refractor, reflector, and compound (or Catadioptric) telescopes. Let's delve into their specifics.

1. **Refractor Telescopes**: These are perhaps what most people picture when thinking of a telescope. Invented by Dutch spectaclemakers in the 17th century, refractor telescopes use a series of lenses to concentrate incoming light at a focal point. They offer sharp images and are excellent for viewing the moon, planets, and other objects within our solar system. However, high-quality refractor models tend to be more expensive and bulkier than other types.

2. **Reflector Telescopes**: Rather than lenses, reflector telescopes use mirrors to gather light. The primary advantage of this design is that mirrors are cheaper and easier to make than lenses, so you can get a larger aperture for the same cost. These telescopes are ideal for faint, deep-sky objects like distant galaxies and nebulae.

3. **Compound Telescopes**: Also known as Catadioptric telescopes, these mix lenses and mirrors to get the best of both worlds. They're portable, versatile, and excellent for viewing a wide variety of celestial objects.

4.3. Choosing Your First Telescope

Selecting a telescope is like buying a car: you should consider what exactly you need it for. Will you be observing from your backyard or traveling to darker sites? Do you want to see the rings of Saturn, explore distant galaxies or dabble in astrophotography? And importantly, what is your budget?

For beginners, a telescope with a wide, stable mount and an aperture of 3 to 5 inches is often a good choice. This size will allow sufficient light gathering to view many of the common celestial objects yet remains portable and easy to use.

4.4. Exploring the Potential of Binoculars

While telescopes are the cornerstone of observational astronomy, one must not overlook the convenience and flexibility of binoculars. They are an ideal choice for the beginner stargazer, as they provide an expansive view of the stars and are generally more intuitive to use than telescopes. Moreover, the viewing through binoculars, with both eyes open, is more comfortable and natural, making it a great tool for extended observation sessions.

When picking binoculars for stargazing, remember that bigger is not always better. The best choice depends on what you wish to look at. For general star-gazing and learning the constellations, a pair of 7x50 or 10x50 binoculars are often the best choice. These numbers denote the magnification power and the aperture size, respectively, and provide a good balance between magnification, brightness, and field of view.

4.5. Fine-tuning Your Experience With Accessories

Your telescope or binoculars can be just the starting point. Accessories can greatly enhance your observing experience by making your instrument more versatile - think of eyepieces, filters, or star charts. Deciding on which accessories to add to your toolbox can be a bit daunting, so here are some commonly used ones:

1. **Eyepieces**: Eyepieces determine the magnification and field of view of your telescope. Adding a set of eyepieces to your collection allows you to customize your viewing experience based on what objects you're looking at.

2. **Filters**: These are great for bringing out the details in certain

objects. For example, a lunar filter reduces the moon's brightness, making it easier to see details in its surface.

3. **Star Charts and Planisphere**: As you learn your way around the sky, these tools can help you locate objects and familiarize you with the constellations.

4. **Barlow lens**: A Barlow Lens effectively doubles or triples the magnification of your current eyepiece, allowing varying views without having to change the eyepiece constantly.

Beginning your astronomical journey can be an exciting but daunting endeavor. However, by selecting appropriate equipment - shaped by your interests, needs, and budget - you can ensure that every starry night provides a doorway to the vastness of our universe. Whether choosing a robust reflector telescope, a versatile pair of binoculars, or opting for additional accessories, remember the purpose is to observe, learn, and find tranquility in the miracles of celestial mechanics. The stars are indeed the limit!

Chapter 5. The Art of Sky Mapping: Navigation through the Heavens

Ready to embark on an interstellar journey? Imagine an expansive sea invigorated with countless islands of hope, each illuminated with a radiant beam of light. No, this is not a vivid portrayal of a terrestrial landscape. We're about to delve into the celestial world up above, where each island symbolizes a star, and crowds of these islands form constellations - our own planetary archipelago.

To begin this adventure, we don't simply gaze up idly; we navigate, we discover, we map. Similar to mariners of old, we map our celestial territory, helping us unveil new perspectives and admire the grandeur of the cosmos. Let's comprehend the art of sky mapping.

5.1. The Basic Framework: Understanding The Celestial Sphere

Picturing the skylight can be mystifying. However, imagine it as a massive celestial sphere with the earth seated at the center—true, an oversimplified model, but functional nonetheless. This cosmos sphere revolved eastward, upturning the majestic array of the celestial bodies.

The celestial equator, imaginatively spreading from Earth's equator, divides the sphere into equal halves. Just like recognizing terrestrial locations, we've longitude and latitude here—Right Ascension (RA) and Declination (Dec) respectively. Remember, these coordinates change due to Earth's axial precession over the years, but it's relatively slow-paced for sky mapping purposes.

5.2. The Signpost constellations and Asterisms

Among the vast stellar canvas, eight-eight official constellations paint a fascinating cosmic story. To get familiar, we begin with recognizing certain 'signpost' constellations and conspicuous asterisms. Not familiar with 'asterisms'? Picture the constellations as cities, and asterisms like landmarks, easy to identify they too loop back to official constellations.

To start with, Northern Hemisphere stargazers can spot the 'Big Dipper,' an asterism in Ursa Major. It's an effective guide to Polaris, 'The North Star,' tailing the Ursa Minor constellation. Southern Hemisphere skywatchers have the Crux, 'The Southern Cross,' for navigational purposes.

5.3. Plotting the Stars: Your Personal Sky Chart

Drawing a reliable sky chart can be an enthralling task. Begin by sketching a basic grid representing the celestial equator (0° Dec) and the local meridian (both horizon limits). Depending on your location and time, add in known constellations, asterisms, and noteworthy celestial bodies. Mention their RA and Dec positions and assign other notable details. Augment your chart with cardinal directions and corresponding altitude degrees.

Remember, a personal sky chart evolves. As your stargazing experience enriches, you may add more galaxies, obscure asterisms, and even learn to predict meteor showers!

5.4. Stargazing Apps Can Be Your Cosmic Compass

In an era of digital connection, why not connect with the cosmos too? Numerous mobile software, like Star Walk, SkyView, or Google Sky Map, offer their portable planetarium. Not only do they provide real-time virtual sky maps, but also alerts for forthcoming space events. However, ensure digital sky gazing doesn't replace your raw cosmic experience.

5.5. Cosmic Calendar: Seasonal Shifts in The Night Sky

Astronomy is patient. Stars and constellations shift their positions with seasons due to Earth's orbit around the sun. For instance, Orion rules the winter skies while Cygnus soars high in summers. Embrace astronomy as a year-round hobby, watch its seasonal variations, and find rhythm in the cosmic clockwork.

5.6. Ancient Skills: The Art of Celestial Navigation

Seafarers of ancient times often used celestial bodies for navigation. Their methods were far from obsolete, as celestial navigation was taught in naval academies until recently. Using a sextant, measuring angular distances between observable bodies, one could quickly determine his coordinates at sea. Implementing similar principles, celestial triangulation or 'celestial fix' can be a fascinating addition to your astronomical journeys!

Navigating the cosmos can be as humbling as it is invigorating. Remember, sky mapping isn't tied to strict principles or accuracy, but inciting curiosity, fostering patience, and enhancing mindfulness. It's this art that connects us to our ancestors, invites inquisitiveness, and forces us to find our humble place in the cosmic theater. So, equip your cosmic compass, turn your gaze upwards, and etch your personal footprints on the canvas of the cosmos.

Chapter 6. A Celestial Calendar: Important Astronomical Events

The sparkling sky overhead is more than just a celestial painting; it's a calendar, revealing the cosmic schedule of our universe. We often feel that the stars are eternal and unchanging, but even they have their moments of drama. Just like, there are times in the Earth's journey around the Sun when we witness astronomical spectacles such as meteor showers, eclipses, and planet parades. This chapter unravels the grandeur of these celestial events, guiding us on a journey through the high points of our year in space.

6.1. The Moon and its Phases

Our closest astronomical body, the Moon, puts on a nightly show of waxing and waning phases. Starting as a tiny sliver of a New Moon emerging from the solar glare, it bulks up night by night until it gleams resplendently as the Full Moon. Each phase of the Moon has a timetable, predictable as a pendulum's swing, allowing for a delightful watch, especially for the novice stargazer.

Month	New Moon	First Quarter	Full Moon	Last Quarter
January	2, 31	8, 24	17	16
February	1, 30	8, 23	16	15
March	2, 31	10, 26	18,	17
April	1, 30	8, 23	16	15
May	1, 30	8, 24	18	18
June	1, 30	8, 24	18	17

Month	New Moon	First Quarter	Full Moon	Last Quarter
July	1, 30	8, 23	16	16
August	1, 30	8, 23	16	15
September	1, 30	8, 23	16	15
October	1, 30	8, 23	16	15
November	1, 30	8, 23	16	15
December	1, 30	8, 23	16	15

Additionally, there are chances to witness lunar eclipses when Earth blocks the sunlight from reaching the Moon, making it disappear or turning it a peculiar shade of red. Meteor showers too can be a conversational spectacle.

6.2. Solar and Lunar Eclipses

Solar and Lunar eclipses are celestial phenomenons that offer some of the most dramatic views in the sky. They occur when the Earth, Moon, and Sun align in such a way that one casts a shadow upon another.

Solar eclipses occur at New Moon, when the Moon passes directly in front of the Sun as seen from a narrow strip on Earth's surface. Lunar eclipses happen at Full Moon when the Moon moves into Earth's shadow. The former is a delicate, rare event, while the latter is more commonly observable from any location on Earth's night side.

The predicted dates for eclipses in the upcoming year are as follows:

Month	Solar Eclipses	Lunar Eclipses
March	3 (Partial)	-

Month	Solar Eclipses	Lunar Eclipses
May	-	8 (Total)
September	16 (Annular)	-
November	-	30 (Partial)

Chapter 7. Meteor Showers

Meteor showers are triggered when Earth crosses the path of a comet, causing debris from the comet to enter Earth's atmosphere where they vaporize and create a flurry of 'shooting stars'. Each shower is named after the constellation from where the meteors seem to originate.

The most famous showers are the Perseids in August and the Geminids in December. Here are the major showers and their dates for next year:

Meteor Shower	Peak Night	Best After
Quadrantids	January 3-4	Midnight
Lyrids	April 21-22	Moonset
Perseids	August 11-12	Moonset
Orionids	October 21-22	Midnight
Leonids	November 17-18	Moonset
Geminids	December 13-14	Sunset

7.1. Conjunctions and Oppositions

Other significant events in space are conjunctions and oppositions, involving the alignment of planets.

A conjunction happens when two or more celestial bodies appear close together in the sky. Opposition is when a planet is in the part of the sky directly opposite the Sun, meaning it is visible from sunset to sunrise.

Here's what to watch out for in the following year:

Month	Conjunctions	Oppositions
January	Jupiter-Saturn (6th)	Mars (19th)
March	Venus-Saturn (6th)	-
May	Jupiter-Venus (10th)	-
July	Saturn-Mars (5th)	-
August	Venus-Mars (15th)	Jupiter (12th)
October	Jupiter-Saturn (21st)	-
December	Mars-Saturn (15th)	-

Stargazing is an eternal journey of discovery and wonder. This celestial calendar, filled with moon phases, eclipses, meteor showers, and more will aid you in this journey, helping you understand the rhythms of the universe and perhaps, learn something about your place in it. As a mindful stargazer, your connection with the cosmos will deepen, and you'll tap into the tranquility that only the night sky can offer.

Chapter 8. The Astronomer's Mind: Mindfulness in the Cosmic Realm

Gazing into the vast expanse of the cosmos, we are often struck by a sense of marvel and mystery. The true beauty of the universe, however, reveals itself not just in what we can see but in the expansiveness of thought and tranquility of mind that this magnificent spectacle incites.

Through the lens of an astronomer, the cosmos doesn't simply exist. Instead, it comes alive, dancing and unfolding its secrets in the tranquil silence of the night. That's the remarkable journey we will embark on together in this chapter. Let's delve deeper into what it means to be not just a watcher of the skies, but a mindful participant in the grand cosmic play of the universe.

8.1. Becoming One with the Cosmos

Let's begin by establishing a bridge between your current perception of the universe and the potential for a heightened, more immersive understanding. It's not so much about a transformation of the mind, but rather an opening up of the heart and the senses.

You see, astronomy is not just a science; it's a form of meditation. And it's through this meditative process – away from the hustle and bustle of daily life – that we can truly appreciate the cosmic spectacle above us.

Try this next time you venture outdoors on a clear, starry night.

Allow yourself to become quiet. Leave the stresses and worries of the day behind you, and make yourself totally present in the now. With every breath you take, envision that you're drawing in the cool tranquility of the cosmos. And as you exhale, imagine releasing all the mental and emotional turbulence that might bubble beneath the surface.

As you become more and more attuned to this rhythmic inflow and outflow of serenity, cast your eyes upward. Try not to bring images, scientific concepts or intellectual thoughts to bear on what you see. Just gaze.

8.2. The Dance of the Stars

As your jangled nerves begin to succumb to the tranquil majesty of the night sky, an interesting shift takes place. No longer a mere spectator, you step onto the cosmic stage as an active participant.

The stars, planets, and galaxies up above are no longer remote and out of reach. They seem closer, more tangible. It's as though the cosmos has come down and enveloped you in its vast embrace. And it's here, in this nurturing celestial cradle, that you begin to dance with the stars.

The constellations don't just slumber in your view, they take center stage, pirouetting through the darkness in a celestial ballet. Each star, each nebula, and each galaxy has its own rhythm and movement in the cosmic waltz. Even the occasional shooting star, hurtling through the infinite realm adds to the grand choreography, a fleeting but enchanting solo performance.

8.3. Cosmic Perspective: Shattering Earthly Limitations

As your dance with the cosmos deepens, the sense of self as separate from everything else begins to blur. The universe is no longer 'out there' while you are 'down here'. Instead, there's a magnificent fusion of you and the universe. The boundary line is dissolved.

The vastness of the cosmos that may seem daunting and perhaps even insignificant at first, transforms into a welcoming realm that invites exploration and self-discovery. And it is within this boundless cosmic expanse that one truly starts appreciating his or her place and perspective in the universe.

Letting go of earthly anchors and biases helps the mind expand and embrace the cosmic perspective. Does this not beckon to the very essence of mindfulness – to be utterly present in the moment, to be fully engaged in the process of living, unfettered by preconceptions and unnecessary mental clutter?

8.4. Astronomy: A Gateway to Enlightenment

In conclusion, astronomy stands as much more than a scientific pursuit. It is a gateway to personal enlightenment, a tool for attaining a state of mindfulness that encompasses not only our individual selves, but the grandeur of the entire universe.

Through mindful stargazing, just as the cosmos reveals itself one star at a time, the layers of self-awareness unfold. We find ourselves slowing down, granting the much-needed space to breathe, to feel, to introspect. It becomes a journey of self-discovery through a cosmic lens, enriching both our understanding of the universe and our place in it.

Grounded in this newfound wisdom, the universe opens its arms to us, offering its mysteries and truths to our curious eyes and open minds. Through our cosmos-tinted glasses, we find peace, tranquility, and a profound sense of unity. It all becomes a dance, an interplay of cosmic energy, in which we are active, mindful participants.

As you cultivate the art of mindful stargazing and deepen your cosmic consciousness, you'll realize that the beauty of the universe goes far beyond the visible. And in pursuing this cosmic harmony, every night under the stars will become a new adventure, a fresh exploration, an extraordinary celestial experience.

Chapter 9. Starlight Meditation: Peace under a Thousand Suns

As you step into the resonating tranquility of the night, allow your gaze to travel upwards, transcending through layers of invisible air to meet the celestial dome speckled with innumerable sources of ancient light. Settle into a comforting position, unwind every muscle, and take a moment to acclimate to your surroundings. This is the beginning of your starlight meditation, a unique blend of mindfulness and stargazing.

9.1. An Invitation to Tranquillity

Start by drawing deep, quenching breaths, allowing your lungs to expand and your body to relax. Each breath acts as an anchor, steadying your heart and mind for the cosmic journey ahead. Through the rhythm of your own increasingly restful state, you begin syncing with the harmonious pulse of the universe.

Feel the insignificance of the worries that crowd your mind as you observe the eternal vastness above. Allow yourself a chance to fully embrace the meditative space under the granite-black canopy, and let the gentle twinkling silence the cacophony of your thoughts.

9.2. Welcoming the Stars

Redirect your attention towards the sparkling dots above. Each star, a conduit of radiant energy, is narrating a millennia-old tale. Notice the different colors, intensities, and patterns—they are a clear testament to the varied composition, temperature, and stages of stars' lifecycles.

As you move your gaze across the sky, visualize the infinite expanse of space that these tiny specks of light have travelled to fall on your receptive eyes. The starlight you see tonight could be a chronicle from a celestial body that existed billions of years ago but has since faded into cosmic oblivion. You're not just observing, but experiencing a visual echo from the past that invites deep tranquility.

9.3. The Celestial Rhythm

It's time now to steer your mindfulness to the orchestrated movements of the heavenly spheres. Celestial bodies may appear stationary to the naked eye but, upon mindful observation, you'll notice a steady change, a celestial dance choreographed by the laws of nature.

Pause to recognize how our relative position to stars changes due to Earth's rotation and revolution. Subtly shifting constellations, the waxing and waning of the Moon, or the dazzling dart of a meteor reveals the remarkable rhythms of night ballet. And as we weave these movements into our mindfulness, we sync our thoughts with the tranquil rhythm of the cosmos.

9.4. Softening into Silence

Now, tether your awareness to the quietude around you. Encased in this celestial silence, there is an elusive music of the universe. You might begin to perceive faint cosmic whispers amidst the profound hush - resonances that have journeyed through interstellar spaces.

As we embrace the silence, we not only create space between ourselves and our thoughts but also put into perspective our position and purpose within the cosmos. For in this silence, we are given a tangible reminder that we are a part of this beautiful complexity that exists above and below us, within and without us.

9.5. Closing the Practice

Conclude your starlight meditation with renewed calmness and a heightened sense of connectivity with the cosmos. Draw a few deep breaths again, anchoring your resurfaced consciousness back to your surroundings.

Remember, the universe isn't outside of you or something to be conquered, but it's an extension of you. It does not end at the farthest reaches of our sight but continues inward, mirroring its expansive, intricate nature within each one of us.

Gently return your gaze back down to Earth, bringing with you the warmth of starlight and cosmic tranquility into your earthly existence. As the boundaries dissolve and the borders melt, what remains is a sense of oneness - a celestial symphony of unity that redefines our understanding of ourselves and our place in the cosmos.

Cherish this newfound connection and harmony that starlight meditation heralds, and let it imbue each of your earthly tasks with serenity and fulfillment. Reflect on the interweave of stargazing and mindfulness as you carry forward this sense of peace and connectivity until your next celestial rendezvous.

9.6. Reflection after the Practice

Let your experience of starlight meditation reverberate in your heart. Reflect and journal any insights received, thoughts unraveled, or emotions stirred during the practice. Honoring your inner experiences in silence under the night sky may just offer an enlightened perspective you had awaited all this long, a realignment of personal energy with the cosmic energy.

Blend this revelation into your day-to-day life and feel how it transforms your relationship with self, others, and the universe. This replenishment is the cosmic gift for the mindful stargazer - tranquil peace under a thousand suns.

Chapter 10. Night Sky Photography: Capturing Stellar Masterpieces

The cosmos is a vast expanse of beauty and mystery, a brilliant canvas painted with celestial bodies. No words can truly express its grandeur, but a picture can attempt to capture a shimmer of its glory. Night sky photography, a skillful blend of science and art, can make this possible. It can capture astronomical objects and landscapes illuminated by them, serving as a tribute to our ceaseless fascination with the night sky.

Embracing night sky photography not only brings out a universe of possibilities but also facilitates your mindful appreciation of the universe, enhancing your relationship with the stellar vault.

10.1. Getting Started

Night sky photography requires patience, practice, and preparation. You're not just taking a snapshot; you're capturing the dynamic beauty of the universe. Therefore, understanding astronomical conditions and patterns is as crucial as mastering technical skills.

First and foremost, you need to know your tools. A Digital Single Lens Reflex (DSLR) or a Mirrorless Interchangeable Lens Camera (MILC) is generally a good choice, owing to their powerful sensors, manual settings, and compatibility with various lenses. A wide-angle lens is a common staple, as it can capture large portions of the sky. In contrast, a telescope can be used for deep-sky photography.

A tripod is non-negotiable- to achieve crisp, clear images, the camera must remain utterly still. Considering long exposures are used in night sky photography, even the smallest vibration could blur your shot. Also, familiarize yourself with a remote shutter release, either wired or wireless, to further remove chances of camera shake.

10.2. Understanding the Sky

A clear, dark sky is the canvas for your stellar masterpiece. Unfortunately, light pollution often hinders our visibility. Hence, great locations are mostly far from city lights, on high grounds, or in deserts or coastal areas. There are numerous dark sky maps available online to help you locate low light pollution sites.

Get acquainted with the concept of astronomical twilight - the period when the sun is far enough below the horizon that light doesn't interfere with stargazing. The darkest skies are offered during the 'new moon' phase, making it the best time for night sky photography.

Understanding celestial movements, seasons, and constellations can greatly enhance your shots. For instance, knowing when the Milky Way's core is most visible can dramatically improve your astro-landscape photography.

10.3. Technical Know-how: Camera Settings

Night sky photography often entails working with settings that are rarely used during daytime photography. You need to venture beyond automatic modes and work primarily with manual settings, which offer you complete control over your camera.

Your ISO setting, which adjusts the camera's sensitivity to light, will generally need to be higher than in regular photography. While a high ISO can introduce noise, many modern cameras can handle ISOs of around 3200 or 6400 quite well.

Exposure time is another crucial factor. The '500 Rule' provides a good starting point - divide 500 by your lens's focal length to determine the longest exposure time before stars appear to trail due to Earth's rotation.

Your aperture has to be set to its widest setting, often denoted as the smallest f-number, to capture as much light as possible.

10.4. Post-processing: The Final Touch

Photos straight out of the camera rarely showcase the night sky as brilliantly as we would hope. Post-processing software like Adobe Lightroom or Photoshop can help enhance the details and vibrant colors of your photos.

Start by reducing noise and correcting lens distortions. Then, adjust the exposure, contrast, highlights, shadows, whites, and blacks to bring out the most details. Work with the color temperature and tint to bring out the cool and warm hues of the sky. You can increase vibrancy and saturation to highlight the colors in your shot.

Yet, post-processing is not just about making changes – it's about doing so responsibly. Keep the natural presentations of celestial objects in mind to retain the authenticity of your frame.

Remember, night sky photography is not about capturing a perfect shot on your first attempt. The process is as significant as the result. Make sure to spend some time simply under the stars, as it is all part of the mindful stargazing journey. By merging the scientific with the creative, you create something more than a photograph. It's an homage to the cosmic powers above and a testament to the human quests below.

Chapter 11. Interstellar Wonders: Nebulae, Galaxies and More

Beyond the ordinary reach of the naked human eye, within the alluring vista of the night sky, reside ethereal landscapes of nebulae, galaxies, and more. These cosmic wonders, invisible yet present, are scattered about in the galactic void and form the foundation of the universe's endless possibilities. In this chapter, we embark on an immersive journey to explore these invisible pieces of wonder and learn more about our larger cosmic neighborhood.

11.1. The Remarkable Nebulae

Within the distant spaces of the cosmos, lies an awe-inspiring marvel of the universe: the nebula. Nebulae are celestial bodies composed of dust, hydrogen, helium, and other ionized gases which are truly a sight to behold. Amid the vast vacuum of space, they form resplendent, multicolored mists that paint the cosmos with breath-taking exquisiteness.

Nebulae are often star-nurseries, breeding grounds where new stars are born and nurtured. These star-forming regions are rich in molecular gas and dust, providing the raw materials needed to bring new stars to life. Their radiant colors tell the tale of their composition, with red typically indicating the presence of hydrogen and blue signifying oxygen.

One spectacular example of a nebula is The Orion Nebula, arguably one of the most well-studied nebulae in human history. Located approximately 1,344 light-years away from Earth, it is visible to the naked eye as the middle "star" in the sword of Orion. It is an active factory for new stars and planetary systems, and like other nebulae, is a vivid example of the universe's continuous cycle of death and creation.

11.2. Diving into Galaxies

Shifting focus from birthplaces of stars, let's now delve into grandiose galaxies—these massive systems of stars, gas, dust, and dark matter present an enchanting spectacle of cosmic art. There are billions of galaxies in the observable universe, each one home to millions, billions, or even trillions of stars. The Milly Way, our very own galactic residence, is just one of them.

Galaxies are grouped into four primary shapes: elliptical, spiral, barred spiral, and irregular. The distinctive spirals, such as our Milky Way, are characterized by curled arms extending from a central bulge, while elliptical galaxies, massive yet shapeless, often contain older stars and less gas and dust. The barred spiral galaxies boast a central bar-shaped structure from which their spiral arms extend, and the irregular counterparts lack any coherent shape, painting a whimsical, disorderly picture in the cosmos.

Galaxies, like grains of sand on a cosmic beach, group together to form clusters and superclusters, guided by invisible hands of gravity. These colossal gatherings are the largest gravitationally bound structures in the observable universe. Amidst all this, our home galaxy, the Milky Way, is part of a group of galaxies called the Local Group, which in turn is part of the Virgo Supercluster.

11.3. Beyond Galaxies: Clusters, Superclusters, and Voids

To grasp the immensity of the universe, let's stray further beyond galaxies. Bound by gravity, galaxies do not stand alone but form intertwined cosmic structures—clusters and superclusters. A galaxy cluster typically comprises hundreds to thousands of galaxies. The gravity holding these galaxies together is so strong that many have temperatures of millions of degrees and contain interstellar mediums composed of hot gas that shines brightly in X-rays.

Superclusters are even more extensive. They are vast assemblies of galaxy clusters and form the most enormous coherent structures in the universe.

Enveloping these structures are cosmic voids—regions with few or even no galaxies. These voids represent gaps in the cosmic web, and yet, they too play a crucial role. Their existence substantiates the existence of dark matter and influences the large-scale structure of the universe.

Herein lie the vast multitudes of interstellar wonders - nebulae, galaxies, clusters, superclusters, and cosmic voids. Each of these celestial structures contributes to the constant ebb and flow of the universe— the cosmic ballet of birth, growth, death, and rebirth. Despite their colossal scales and mind-bending complexity, these celestial wonders are interconnected and integral to the universe's existence.

In conclusion, the universe we inhabit is as beautiful as it is vast. Its endless expanse, dotted with celestial bodies and brilliant lights, invites us to indulge in stargazing and astral contemplation. Through the exploration of nebulae, galaxies, and cosmic structures, we realize that we are a small yet integral part of the boundless cosmic dance of the universe—a dance of stars, of lights, of life— that isn't just out there in the void, but also within us, reminding us subtly of our cosmic connection.

Chapter 12. Stargazing as a Lifestyle: Fostering a Lifelong Hobby

The excitement of observing that first celestial body through a telescope or even your naked eyes is unparalleled. Over time, however, stargazing can progress from an exciting curiosity to a lifestyle that is surprisingly ingrained in mindfulness and is a lifelong hobby worth nurturing.

12.1. The Lure of the Night Sky

Night has fired human imagination from time immemorial. Beyond the artificial city lights, the panoramic night sky emerges in all its grandeur, popping with stellar gems that twinkle in a voyeuristic ballet. Stargazing, as the name suggests, allows us to peek into these celestial extravaganzas, many of them light-years away, one star at a time. Embracing it as a lifestyle places us on a path of constant discovery, mindfulness, and learning.

12.2. Tools for Your Journey

A star chart or a planetarium software like Stellarium, a telescope, and a willing heart, are the fundamental tools for a stargazer. But remember, the most potent instrument is your curiosity. Binoculars offer a fabulous tool for beginners because of their easy handling and lower costs. As you foster this hobby, telescopes of increasing complexity will amplify your exploration, extending your reach to distant galaxies and nebulae.

12.3. Cultivating the Art of Patient Observation

Observing the night sky isn't about fleeting, cursory glances. Drawing from mindfulness, the discipline encourages slow, contemplative engagement. Take time to see the gradation of stars, the distinct color of Mars, or the rings of Saturn. The key is to focus your attention on individual objects, patiently observing their details and losing yourself in sweeping cosmic panoramas.

12.4. Understanding and Appreciating Our Cosmic Home

The more you gaze at the night sky, the more you foster an understanding and appreciation of our place in the cosmos. This cognizance turns mundane nightly observations into a practice of cosmic mindfulness. Tracking the paths of planets or noting the phases of the moon fosters a deeper connection with our universe. Your hobby suddenly weaves a profound narrative of your existence in a cosmic ballet that has been taking place for billions of years.

12.5. Nightly Routines and Log Keeping

A great way to nurture stargazing as a lifestyle is establishing nightly routines and logging observations. This activity doesn't just reflect commitment but also aids learning. Keeping track of the sky's behavior, jotting down dates of meteor showers or eclipses, or sketching an awe-inspiring nebula you observed can make your hobby more rewarding. Adopting these routines develops resilience, patience, and the joy of finding order in apparent chaos.

12.6. Stargazing as a Social Activity

While stargazing can be a solitary endeavor, socializing it can make the experience more fun. Join a local astronomy club or attend star parties — it provides a platform to share experiences, learn from others, and nurture a sense of a shared cosmic home. Learning from seasoned observers can boost your knowledge and fuel your passion for the stars.

12.7. Enduring the Hurdles

Like all hobbies turned into lifestyles, stargazing comes with its hurdles: cloudy nights, light pollution, or equipment issues. But embrace these as part of the journey. Think of cloudy nights as opportunities to learn more about cloud patterns. Engage in advocacy for dark skies against light pollution. Tweaking and understanding the nuances of your equipment can be as much a part of the hobby as the observation itself.

12.8. Celestial Events: Anchoring Time and Space

Every so often, the cosmos offers front-row tickets to spectacular events - meteor showers shooting across the sky, brilliant comets sweeping past, or rare alignments of planets. These events punctuate our daily lives with the mysteries of space and time. Waiting for them, observing them, notching them on the timeline of your life, further anchors this hobby into your lifestyle.

12.9. The Health Benefits of Stargazing

The act of staring up, concentrating on the celestial, is proven to evoke a meditative state. The tranquility and peace intertwined in the practice of stargazing yield significant mental health benefits. It instills a sense of calm, helps manage stress, and can be a unique form of meditation.

12.10. Stargazing as a Life-Long Journey

Stargazing, when embraced as a lifestyle, becomes a life-long journey. Our universe, a grand opera of cosmic bodies in continuous motion, ensures that each look at the night sky is unique. It presents an infinite learning curve and a lifetime of tranquil moments under the stars.

In conclusion, adopting stargazing as a lifestyle isn't just about following the stars. It's about fostering a deep-rooted connection with our universe; it's about nurturing a lifelong hobby that brings peace, knowledge, and perspective. So, let the stars guide you, calm you, and inspire you.